CW01183716

Original title:
Starlit Shadows

Copyright © 2024 Swan Charm
All rights reserved.

Author: Mirell Mesipuu
ISBN HARDBACK: 978-9908-1-0679-3
ISBN PAPERBACK: 978-9908-1-0680-9
ISBN EBOOK: 978-9908-1-0681-6

Glowing Trails of Starlight

In the night, the stars align,
Dancing lights, a festive sign.
Whispers of joy, the breezes share,
Laughter lifted, floating air.

Candles flicker with gentle grace,
Each flame shines in its own place.
Friends gather 'neath a painted sky,
Wishing dreams on stars that fly.

Celestial Murmurs at Dusk

As day fades into velvet hue,
The world awakens, fresh and new.
Crickets sing in harmony,
Soft notes echo, wild and free.

Moonlight dances on silver streams,
Painting the night in vibrant dreams.
Voices blend in cheerful songs,
A festivity where joy belongs.

Reflections in the Glistening Dark

Reflections shimmer on calm, crisp lakes,
Waves of laughter, wherever one makes.
The night embraces, warm and bright,
Stars twinkle with pure delight.

Glasses raised, a clink, a cheer,
In every heart, warmth draws near.
Together we weave this joyful night,
In glistening dark, everything feels right.

Enchanted by Night's Glow

In the hush of the evening tide,
Magic swells, we feel the ride.
Lanterns softly light the way,
Guiding souls on this joyous play.

Hearts entwined in laughter bright,
Dancing shadows swirl in light.
With every step, the night ignites,
An enchanted world of festive sights.

Celestial Whispers in the Dusk

Underneath the twilight sky,
Silhouettes dance, spirits fly.
Stars like gems begin to gleam,
Echoing every joyful dream.

Laughter twirls in gentle breeze,
Carried softly through the trees.
Magic weaves through every sound,
In this wonder, joy is found.

Candles flicker, shadows sway,
As we celebrate this day.
Whispers sweet, the moonlight glows,
Bringing warmth wherever it goes.

With every cheer, our hearts ignite,
In this glow, the world feels right.
Together, we embrace the night,
In festive hues of pure delight.

Velvet Hues of the Cosmic Horizon

In the hush of evening's grace,
Stars adorn the velvet space.
Colors dance upon the ground,
Radiance in joy is found.

Beneath the cosmic tapestry,
We laugh, we sing, we're wild and free.
The universe shares its glow,
A vibrant pulse, a steady flow.

With every shimmer, hope ignites,
Entertainment in the nights.
People gather, voices rise,
Hearts united, reaching skies.

Blessed moments weave the air,
A celebration everywhere.
In this realm of cosmic bliss,
We find our place, we find our kiss.

Radiant Secrets in the Abyss

Deep within the ocean's heart,
Luminous dreams begin to start.
Upward bubbles surf the gloom,
Curious lights in swirling bloom.

Festive whispers in the deep,
Secrets of the night we keep.
Waves like ribbons, soft and bright,
Hiding treasures in the night.

Every splash a joyful song,
Echoing where we belong.
In the depths, we brightly shine,
Creating magic, yours and mine.

Swaying with the ebb and flow,
In the dark, our spirits glow.
Together, we explore the sea,
Celebrating wild and free.

Murmurs of Hidden Lights

Underneath the starry dome,
Nature sings its ancient poem.
Fireflies flit, a dazzling show,
Whispers of joy begin to flow.

In the stillness, dreams take flight,
Painting stories in the night.
Colors burst, a vivid spree,
Carried forth on winds of glee.

Gather round, let spirits soar,
In this glow, we seek for more.
Laughter echoes, hearts entwined,
In this bliss, true love we find.

With every cheer, joy's a delight,
Murmurs shared, a pure invite.
In the night, we shine so bright,
Creating memories in the light.

Radiance Beyond the Midnight Realm

Stars twinkle bright in the deep dark sky,
Laughter and joy, as the moments fly.
Candles aglow, a welcoming sight,
Hearts filled with warmth, a magical night.

Music and dance under shimmering light,
Footsteps of bliss in a soft moonlight.
Together we gather, our spirits set free,
In this festive realm, it's just you and me.

Colors like rainbows, painting the air,
Each memory crafted with laughter to share.
Sparkles of dreams in the night we embrace,
An eternal bond in this joyful place.

Ethereal Glows of Dusk

As the sun dips low, the hues start to blend,
With whispers of twilight, our hearts start to mend.
Lanterns ignited, they dance in the breeze,
A night filled with magic, a moment to seize.

Chorus of crickets, a soft serenade,
Under the canopy, memories are made.
Joyful celebrations with friends all around,
In the essence of dusk, true bliss can be found.

Fireflies flicker like dreams come alive,
In this festive time, our souls start to thrive.
Hand in hand, we sway, lost in delight,
Embracing the beauty of this enchanting night.

Echoes of Light in the Dark

Glistening shadows, where whispers reside,
The echoes of laughter float soft on the tide.
Glowing together, our spirits align,
With every heartbeat, this magic is mine.

Voices of joy spread like stars in the air,
Creating a tapestry of love everywhere.
Moments like petals, they drift and they sway,
In the echoes of light, we dance and we play.

Cups raised in cheer, to the night we adore,
Every spark ignites, leaving us wanting more.
In shadows we find, a vibrant delight,
As we weave through the fabric of this festive night.

Nighttime's Embrace

Moonlight drapes softly, a shimmering shawl,
In the warmth of the night, we find our all.
Laughter resounds in the cool evening air,
A gathering of souls, responsive and rare.

As lanterns flicker, their glow draws us near,
Wrapped in the magic, there's nothing to fear.
Together we forge, memories bright and clear,
In the embrace of the night, joy is sincere.

The rhythm of hearts, like a dance, they entwine,
Each beat a reminder, our love's truly divine.
And as stars unveil their celestial grace,
We revel in nighttime's warm, gentle embrace.

Illuminated Silhouettes

Dancing shadows twirl and play,
Beneath bright lights of blue and gray.
Laughter echoes, hearts ignite,
In this wondrous, vivid night.

Colorful streams flow through the air,
Filling souls with warmth and care.
Sparkling dreams take flight and soar,
We'll share our joy forevermore.

Each corner bursts with joyous cheer,
As festive faces draw us near.
With every smile, a memory grows,
In the glow, our happiness shows.

Together we twine in vibrant hues,
Under the skies of rich, deep blues.
Our illuminated silhouettes gleam,
As we dance within the dream.

Serenity Beneath the Night Sky

Stars flicker gently, setting the tone,
Whispers of night with a subtle drone.
Moonlight spills on the grassy floor,
A calm embrace, we always adore.

Night blooms soft in silver and gold,
Stories of magic waiting to unfold.
Breaths are taken, all worries cease,
In this realm of quiet peace.

Fireflies waltz in delicate flight,
We find our place in this serene night.
Each heartbeat syncs with the soft breeze,
Moments like these put our minds at ease.

As we gaze up into the vast sky,
Harmony reigns, and spirits fly.
Under the stars, our hopes collide,
In this tranquility, we abide.

Phantom Light and Glistening Hope

A flicker dances, a phantom's wink,
Glimmers of joy make our spirits sink.
In the hush of night, the magic unfolds,
Glistening hopes turning dreams into gold.

Waves of laughter ripple and spin,
Encouragement flows from within.
Each moment a treasure, bright and rare,
In the shadows, we nurture care.

The air is rich with a fragrant tease,
Buds of promise in the gentle breeze.
With every heartbeat in tranquil light,
We chase away darkness, welcoming bright.

Together we shine through playful streams,
Echoing whispers, and vibrant dreams.
In the stillness, our spirits rise,
Bathed in hope beneath starry skies.

The Nocturnal Serenade

Voices sing in the moonlit glow,
Echoes of tales only night could know.
Strings of laughter drift like the breeze,
In this serenade, we find our ease.

Glistening shadows move with delight,
Pulling together in festive flight.
Every note rings through the air,
Inviting all to shed their care.

Under the canopy, dreams intertwine,
Rhythms and memories beautifully align.
With each beat, our hearts keep pace,
In this nocturnal musical embrace.

As stars wink down with a knowing glance,
We revel together in this sweet dance.
In the serenade, we become whole,
A night of passion igniting our soul.

Echoes of the Cosmic Breeze

Stars twinkle in the night, so bright,
Whispers of joy take flight,
Galaxies spin with delight,
In a festival of light.

Colors burst in the sky,
Banners wave, spirits fly,
Laughter echoes, spirits sigh,
As we dance, time slips by.

Sparkling laughter fills the air,
Every heart, a vibrant flare,
Unity bound by our care,
In this moment, we all share.

Dreams unfold, stories told,
Magic in the night's gold,
In this joy, we never grow old,
Together, our hearts uphold.

Where Shadows Meet the Light

In the twilight's gentle glow,
Mysteries begin to flow,
Where whispers start to grow,
A dance of shadows, soft and slow.

Hope ignites with each star,
Close your eyes, feel the spar,
Connections form, near and far,
Together, we are who we are.

With every heartbeat, we shine,
In this circle, you're divine,
Embracing moments that entwine,
As the darkness starts to decline.

Hands are raised to the night,
As we bask in pure delight,
For in unity, we find light,
Together, our dreams take flight.

The Hidden Realm of Illumination

In a garden where dreams bloom,
Colors chase away the gloom,
Every petal, a sweet perfume,
Illuminated by the moon.

Whispers dance upon the breeze,
Songs of joy among the trees,
Life's rhythm brings us to our knees,
In this realm, we find our ease.

Chasing shadows with delight,
As the stars ignite the night,
With each heartbeat, we take flight,
In this haven, all feels right.

With vibrant hues and soft embrace,
Together, we'll find our place,
In this dance, no need to race,
As we smile in love's grace.

Dance with the Night's Canvas

The canvas of night unfurls wide,
As starlight becomes our guide,
With every heartbeat, dreams collide,
In this wonder, there's no pride.

Colors swirl, a lively spin,
Stories told through leaps and grins,
Celebrate where joy begins,
In this dance, the night wins.

Laughter echoes, bright and clear,
Join the magic, feel no fear,
In this moment, we all cheer,
Together, we will persevere.

Beneath the moon's silver sheen,
In the glow, we find the keen,
Hands held tight, forever seen,
As we paint life's festive scene.

Whispers of the Celestial Night

Stars twinkle bright, in joyous delight,
The moon glows softly, bathing all in light.
Laughter dances high, on a gentle breeze,
As shadows play games, beneath the trees.

Fireflies ignite, like diamonds in flight,
Each flicker a wish, in the warm summer night.
Voices rise, swelling, in harmony pure,
Together we celebrate, of that we are sure.

Sipping on dreams, like sweet, sparkling wine,
With hearts intertwined, our spirits align.
In laughter we gather, united as one,
Beneath the vast sky, celebrating the sun.

As the night deepens, our worries take flight,
In the arms of the stars, everything feels right.
We cherish this magic, this beautiful sight,
In whispers of joy, of the celestial night.

Echoes in the Dark

Dancing shadows sway, in a rhythmic embrace,
Each echo a whisper, as hearts interlace.
Faint laughter resounds, through the cool evening air,
Festivities flourish, in love we all share.

Candles flicker gently, casting warmth all around,
As dreams take their flight, to the festive sound.
Underneath the stars, all spirits ignite,
With echoing joy, we gather tonight.

Joyous smiles glow, like the brightest of lamps,
Happiness drifts, in soft, twinkling camps.
Together we weave, in this night so stark,
A tapestry vibrant, with echoes in the dark.

The world feels alive, with enchanting allure,
As dreams intertwine, and joy feels so pure.
In the quiet of night, our laughter embarks,
In the echoes we share, under moonlit arcs.

Silhouettes Beneath the Cosmic Veil

Beneath the vast sky, silhouettes arise,
In the shimmer of stars, we gaze with wide eyes.
The laughter erupts, like a delightfully sweet song,
Each moment a treasure, where we all belong.

In this twilight glow, secrets gently collide,
As dreams twist and swirl, in the cosmic tide.
With every heartbeat, a melody calls,
As we sway together, where wonder enthralls.

The whispers of night, cradle us close,
With every shared tale, our hearts they engross.
As shadows stretch long, in a playful parade,
We dance with the stars, unafraid and unmade.

Under the night sky, we shed every chain,
In the embrace of the cosmos, our joy is our gain.
We twirl through the dreams, in this magical tale,
Together we shine, silhouettes beneath the veil.

Luminescent Dreams of Midnight

A tapestry glows, with colors so bright,
In the hush of the hour, chasing away fright.
Soft whispers of hope, invite us to play,
In luminous realms, where dreams gently sway.

Stars twirl like dancers, around us they beam,
In the depths of the night, we follow the dream.
With laughter as music, our spirits take flight,
In the glow of the moon, everything feels right.

The warmth of the fire, cradles our hearts,
As stories emerge, and adventure departs.
Every flicker of light, writes tales in the dark,
With luminescent dreams, igniting our spark.

Beneath midnight's hush, we gather as one,
Crafting memories bright, until the night's done.
In this joyous embrace, dreams shimmer and play,
In the magic of midnight, we dance and we sway.

Dreams on the Edge of Starlight

In a garden where fireflies dance,
Laughter echoes, seizing a chance.
Twinkling wishes drift on the breeze,
As each heart sways among the trees.

Candles glow softly, casting a spell,
Whispers of joy in a magical well.
Faces aglow, smiles bright as the moon,
We gather together, the night ending soon.

Songs of delight weave through the air,
Every moment a treasure to share.
On the edge of starlight, we stand,
Creating our dreams, hand in hand.

With the cosmos above, a tapestry grand,
We dance to the rhythm, heartbeats unplanned.
In this festive night, we lose all our cares,
As the universe shines and the magic ensnares.

Lullabies of the Cosmic Night

Under a blanket of shimmering stars,
The cosmos sings from afar.
Dreams weave gently, tender and light,
In the lullabies of the cosmic night.

Children of wonder gaze in awe,
As comets streak, enchanting the law.
Festive colors explode in the dark,
Painting the heavens with exuberant spark.

Whispers of stories, of legends long gone,
Float on the wind, like a melodious dawn.
In this realm where hopes ignite,
The universe cradles us, holding us tight.

Together we sway in celestial gleam,
Lost in the magic, caught in a dream.
The night is alive, our spirits take flight,
Melodies resound in the cosmic night.

Wandering Through Moonlit Haze

Wrapped in a blanket of silver and blue,
We wander the pathways, just me and you.
Moonlight dances on leaves, a festive display,
As shadows and whispers lead us astray.

Each step we take is a rhythm divine,
In the hush of the night, our hearts intertwine.
With laughter like bells, we float through the trees,
Carving our tales in the soft, fragrant breeze.

Stars above twinkle like diamonds in air,
Guiding our journey with tender, sweet care.
In the haze of the evening, adventures await,
Together we'll weave every twist of fate.

Through moonlit paths, we dance with delight,
Every heartbeat a promise, everything feels right.
Lost in this moment, carefree and dazed,
Wandering forever through moonlit haze.

The Mystique of Twilight's Embrace

As twilight descends in a hushed, warm glow,
The world celebrates in a magical flow.
Colors of crimson and lavender swirl,
In the festive embrace where dreams unfurl.

Crickets serenade with their gentle hum,
As laughter erupts and the night starts to drum.
Mirthful spirits take flight on the breeze,
In the mystique of twilight, we find our ease.

Candles are lit, glowing bright like our dreams,
We share whispered secrets, unraveling schemes.
The sky blazes with hues, a canvas so wide,
In this moment together, we take it in stride.

With dance in our hearts, we twirl and we sway,
Lost in the magic of twilight's ballet.
In this festive hour, the world feels so right,
Warm in the mystique of the magical night.

Allure of the Midnight Glow

The stars ignite the velvet sky,
A dance of light, the night draws nigh.
Laughter echoes through the trees,
As joy is carried by the breeze.

Anticipation fills the air,
With glimmering eyes, we stop and stare.
A feast of dreams, all bright and bold,
In the allure of stories told.

Candles flicker, casting shades,
Memories woven in masquerades.
Voices merge in harmony,
Beneath the moon, we're wild and free.

The midnight glow, a sweet embrace,
In every heart, a sacred space.
Together still, through laughter's ring,
We celebrate the warmth we bring.

Celestial Lullabies in Twilight

Twilight whispers a soft refrain,
While shadows twinkle like summer rain.
Gentle winds sing through the night,
As dreams take flight on silver light.

Each star a note in the vast expanse,
They beckon us into a cosmic dance.
The moon, our guardian, bright and clear,
Cradles secrets we hold so dear.

Underneath this celestial dome,
We weave our wishes, find our home.
In lullabies that drift and sway,
The night unfolds, and dreams convey.

With every heartbeat, we embrace,
The magic found in this shared space.
In twilight's glow, the world feels right,
As we dissolve in starlit night.

The Mysteries Hidden in Light's Embrace

Glimmers peek from hinterlands,
Magic weaves through soft, warm hands.
In the glow of lanterns, stories breathe,
Mysteries whispered amidst the leaves.

Dancing shadows on cobblestone,
Echoes linger in twilight's tone.
Footsteps tap to an ancient beat,
As joy compels our hearts to meet.

With every flicker, secrets twine,
Creating bonds where stars align.
The night unveils its silent grace,
Warmly held in light's embrace.

In every glint, hope finds its way,
Celebrating life in grand display.
From dusk till dawn, we'll chase the spark,
Illuminated whispers in the dark.

Hushed Reflections of the Night

Softly glows the night aglow,
A realm where dreams and shadows flow.
Beneath the starlit canopy,
Whispers dance in sweet harmony.

In the silence, joy takes flight,
Every heartbeat feels so right.
The moon, a guide through paths unknown,
Fills our hearts, we're never alone.

Glimmers of laughter, moments shared,
In every soul, love's thread is bared.
We gather close, in secret sighs,
Hushed reflections in the skies.

With the dawn, our memories cling,
In the twilight where spirits sing.
As stars awaken from their dreams,
The night embraces all it seems.

Ghosts of a Glittering Sky

Beneath stars that twinkle bright,
Laughter dances through the night.
Joyous whispers fill the air,
Magic sparkles everywhere.

Fireworks bloom like flowers rare,
Bells are ringing, hearts laid bare.
People gather, spirits high,
As dreams take flight in the sky.

Candles flicker, shadows play,
Colors splash in grand array.
Every moment, pure delight,
Glow of friendship, shining bright.

So let the world come alive,
In this joy, we all will thrive.
Let the ghosts of laughter soar,
In our hearts forevermore.

Nightfall's Enigmatic Embrace

As twilight weaves a velvet cloak,
The world unfolds with each soft stroke.
Wonders whisper through the trees,
Carried lightly on the breeze.

In the garden, lanterns glow,
Casting dreams that ebb and flow.
Laughter mingles, love's sweet song,
In this moment, we belong.

Beneath the stars' enchanting light,
Everything feels so right tonight.
The dance begins with graceful sway,
As shadows chase the dusk away.

Friendship warms these cool, crisp hours,
Each connection blooming flowers.
With each heartbeat, memories trace,
Nightfall's sweet and soft embrace.

Secrets of the Stellar Abyss

In the cosmos, secrets lie,
Twinkling bright against the sky.
With each star that shines above,
Whispers echo tales of love.

Underneath the vast expanse,
Moonlight sets the world to dance.
Constellations guide our hearts,
As the universe imparts.

Every spark, a wish that's made,
In this night, fears start to fade.
Gather close, share your delight,
Let the magic take its flight.

As we gaze into the night,
Hearts united, pure and bright.
In the depths, we find our bliss,
Secrets lost in starlit kiss.

Twilight's Veiled Reverie

The sun dips low with colors warm,
Twilight wraps us in its charm.
Balloons float amidst the cheers,
Joyful laughter fills our ears.

With each moment, spirits soar,
Friends gather, craving more.
In this place where dreams ignite,
Every heart beats with delight.

Candles glow and shadows dance,
Life unfolds in vibrant chance.
Underneath the glowing sky,
Let your worries drift and fly.

Embrace this night, our souls entwine,
Every heartbeat, pure divine.
In the magic, we believe,
Twilight's veiled dreams, we conceive.

Light Shimmers in the Dark

In the glow of lanterns bright,
Laughter dances in the night.
Songs of joy fill the warm air,
Magic sparkles everywhere.

Choruses of hearts collide,
As the stars begin to guide.
Dreams are woven, tales are spun,
Underneath the setting sun.

Colors burst with every cheer,
Memories made, drawing near.
Hands entwined, spirits soar,
Together we will dance once more.

Light will shimmer, shadows fade,
In this moment, dreams are laid.
Celebrate with love and grace,
Every smile finds its place.

Celestial Embraces of the Night

Stars will waltz in sky's embrace,
Moonlight spills with gentle face.
Whispers float on silver beams,
Filling hearts with tender dreams.

Dancing shadows, soft and light,
Hold us close through velvet night.
Laughter rings, sweet and clear,
In this realm where love draws near.

Crickets sing their lullaby,
While the world begins to sigh.
Every heartbeat a delight,
In the celestial delight.

Hands reach out to touch the stars,
In this moment, free from scars.
Together under night's embrace,
Feel the magic, taste the grace.

Twilight's Whispering Secrets

Twilight glows with pastel hue,
Inviting whispers, fresh and new.
Nature breathes a soft refrain,
Echoes of the day's sweet pain.

Fireflies dance in gentle streams,
Filling hearts with softest dreams.
Each moment shines like dew-kissed grass,
As the evening hours pass.

Golden sun bids fond farewell,
Stars awake, their stories tell.
In this hush, we find our way,
Crafting memories that will stay.

Hold my hand, let's wander free,
Through twilight's lush tapestry.
Every secret, every sigh,
Kisses softly, like the sky.

Radiant Reveries in Moonbeam's Touch

Moonbeams drip from silver skies,
Painting dreams in soft replies.
Night unfolds its velvet arms,
Cradling all with gentle charms.

Laughter rings like bells at play,
In the magic of the sway.
Every heartbeat, every glance,
Invokes the stars to join our dance.

Radiance glimmers on each face,
In this pure, warm, loving space.
As whispers weave through the air,
Joyful spirits linger there.

With each twinkle, hopes arise,
Beneath the vast and starry skies.
Let's embrace this night so fine,
In radiant dreams, forever shine.

Soft Luminance of Forgotten Echoes

Twinkling glimmers dance on the floor,
Whispers of laughter, tales from before.
Golden threads in the twilight air,
Hearts intertwine in the joy we share.

Candles sparkle with stories untold,
In every flicker, warmth to behold.
Voices uplift in a melodious hum,
As we gather 'round, the night's become.

Chiming bells ring in the sweet refrain,
Echoes of love, erasing the pain.
Soft shadows play on the walls so bright,
Filling the spirit, igniting the night.

Beneath the stars, our dreams take flight,
In the soft luminance, hearts feel light.
Each moment cherished, an eternal glow,
In the festive air, our spirits flow.

Chiaroscuro of the Celestial Sphere

Lights collide in a playful embrace,
A canvas of color, a cosmic space.
Moonlight shimmers on the soft, cold ground,
In this chiaroscuro, joy is found.

Laughter rises with the evening breeze,
Whispers of wishes drift through the trees.
Every star twinkles with promises made,
In the celestial dance, our fears fade.

Colors blend in a radiant swirl,
As the festival of lights begins to unfurl.
Hope ignites in the darkened sky,
In the beauty of night, our spirits fly.

With each shadow, new wonders arise,
In this canvas of dreams, we realize.
Harmony lingers in the air we breathe,
In the magical realm, our souls reprieve.

Rituals of Light and Shade

Dancing flames in soft, flickering hues,
Every heartbeat syncs with the muse.
Songs of joy fill the lengthening night,
In the glow of candles, everything feels right.

Rituals echo through the twilight glow,
Moments immortal, whispers flow.
Beneath garlands of shimmering light,
We weave our dreams in the festive night.

With open arms, the night we greet,
In shadows we find our love's heartbeat.
Happiness, boundless, in every hand held,
In each shared glance, our worries quelled.

Voices harmonize in jubilant cheer,
Filling the world with the warmth we hold dear.
In this sacred space, let light invade,
Through the rituals of love, we are laid.

Celestial Murmurs in the Gloom

In the cool embrace of the starry night,
Celestial murmurs bring pure delight.
Gleaming orbs whisper secrets of old,
In shadows adorned with stories told.

Gathered close in a circle of light,
We share our wishes, hearts taking flight.
The moon softly smiles on our joyful spree,
As laughter echoes through the vast, dark sea.

Every flicker unveils our shared fate,
In this vibrant night, we celebrate.
Together we shine, igniting the gloom,
In the celestial glow, love continues to bloom.

As the night dances to an ancient tune,
Magic ignites under the watchful moon.
With hands joined, we embrace the hour,
In celestial murmurs, we find our power.

Twilight's Gentle Glow

As twilight paints the sky so bright,
The world awakens to soft light.
Laughter echoes through the air,
As joyful hearts find time to share.

String lights dance in festive cheer,
Filling each moment with love near.
Friends gather, smiles all around,
In this warmth, true joy is found.

Chimes of music sweetly play,
Inviting dreams to drift and sway.
Beneath the stars, we sing our song,
In this twilight, we all belong.

Fleeting Dreams of the Night

In the shimmer of night's embrace,
We weave our tales in this sacred space.
Whispers of laughter fill the air,
As hopes and dreams dance everywhere.

Fireflies flicker, a waltz so bright,
Guiding the path through the velvety night.
With every heartbeat, spirits rise,
Underneath the tapestry of skies.

A toast to moments, fleeting yet true,
Memories made, old and new.
In this magic, we hold on tight,
Fleeting dreams fill the heart tonight.

Luminance Beneath the Canopy

Beneath the canopy of the trees,
We gather round, feeling the breeze.
Soft lights glisten like stars above,
Capturing the essence of love.

The night unfolds with stories to tell,
In the warmth of friendship, we dwell.
Laughter dances on every tongue,
Until the joy of living is sung.

Bonfires crackle, sparks take flight,
Illuminating dreams in the night.
Each moment shared adds to the glow,
In this haven, our spirits grow.

The Dance of Stars and Silence

In the hush of night, stars take the stage,
Illuminating beauty, a wondrous page.
We twirl and spin in the moonlight's grace,
Finding our rhythm, a joyful trace.

The silence holds secrets, deep and rare,
As we sway to the music in the air.
With every step, our hearts ignite,
In the dance of stars, we take flight.

Embracing the night with spirits so free,
Together we create sweet harmony.
In this moment, we feel alive,
In the dance of silence, we thrive.

Cosmic Secrets Beneath the Stars

Under the cosmos, laughter flies,
Whispers of stardust fill the skies.
Colors sparkling in the night,
Together, we dance in pure delight.

Galaxies twirl, a grand ballet,
We celebrate night, chasing gray away.
Each twinkle tells a tale so bright,
Embracing the magic, hearts in flight.

With friends around, our spirits soar,
Every secret shared, we crave more.
In this celestial, vibrant play,
Moments cherished, forever will stay.

So let us toast to dreams anew,
Beneath the stars, dreams come true.
In harmony, we sing and cheer,
Cosmic secrets, forever near.

Echoing Light Through the Night

Moonlit echoes dance on waves,
Notes of laughter, the joy it saves.
Fires flicker, stories unfold,
Memories shared, a treasure of gold.

Candles flicker in the softest breeze,
Warm embraces put our hearts at ease.
With every glow, our wishes ignite,
Echoing laughter, a pure delight.

The sky above, a tapestry bright,
Bringing warmth in the cool of night.
Through every shadow, light prevails,
With love in our hearts, we set our sails.

As stars above begin to play,
We treasure this bliss, come what may.
In this moment, so pure and right,
We gather joy, echoing light.

Dappled Dreams in the Moonlight

In the garden where moonbeams kiss,
We weave our dreams in a night of bliss.
Dappled shadows, soft and free,
Paint the world in sweet harmony.

Petals whisper secrets, so divine,
Guided by stars, our hearts entwine.
With every laugh, we bloom like flowers,
Time stands still in these magical hours.

The fragrance of joy in the cooling air,
Together we rise, a vibrant flare.
With twinkling eyes and hearts so light,
We dance through dreams in the soft moonlight.

These fleeting moments, we hold them dear,
Each one a treasure, each smile sincere.
In the dappled glow, our spirits gleam,
Caught in the magic of a moonlit dream.

Beyond the Horizon of Darkness

When shadows linger, hope shines bright,
  We gather courage, hearts in flight.
  With every dawn, a brand new start,
    Together we weave, hand in heart.

Beneath the stars, our spirits sing,
    United in joy, a radiant ring.
    We rise together, hand in hand,
Building a dreamland, vast and grand.

Through every struggle, we find our way,
  Chasing the darkness, welcoming day.
    In laughter's echo, our fears release,
Embracing the warmth, we find our peace.

Beyond the horizon, a promise lies,
  Filled with adventure painted in skies.
With hearts ablaze, we'll chase the light,
  Together we stand, strong and bright.

Silhouettes of Hidden Dreams

In the glow of dusk, whispers rise,
Laughter dances under painted skies.
Colors explode, hopes take flight,
Magic awakens, igniting the night.

Balloons float high, dreams intertwine,
Stars glimmer softly, sweet and divine.
Children's giggles echo in the air,
A tapestry woven with love and care.

Candles flicker in picturesque rows,
Every heartbeat in sync with the prose.
Joyous moments, memories blend,
In this celebration, wonders extend.

As twilight beckons, we raise our cheers,
Together we cherish, banish our fears.
With hearts united, we dance and sway,
In silhouettes bright, we'll find our way.

Shadows Found in Celestial Streams

Under a canopy of shimmering stars,
We gather beneath, forgetting our scars.
The moonlight sparkles on shimmering streams,
Each ripple a whisper of hidden dreams.

Festive laughter fills the cool night air,
A carnival spirit, joy everywhere.
With every step, shadows come alive,
In harmony's dance, together we thrive.

Guided by fireflies, glowing and free,
They illuminate paths for you and me.
Under starry skies, we sing our song,
In this celestial embrace, we belong.

The night wraps us close, a warm, sweet embrace,
In whispers of friendship, we find our place.
Shadows and dreams weave a glorious seam,
Celebrating life in celestial streams.

The Enchantment of Nightfall

As daylight falters, the magic awakes,
Fireworks burst, the whole world shakes.
Colors cascade, igniting the sky,
In the enchantment of nightfall, we fly.

Music flows gently, like a sweet sigh,
Memories twinkle, a soft lullaby.
With every heartbeat, the rhythm grows strong,
In this twilight realm, we all belong.

The world dressed in sparkles, glimmers of gold,
Stories of old, in new tales retold.
We gather as one, hearts open wide,
In the enchantment, we all take pride.

A dance in the moonlight, a laughter-filled spree,
Wishing on stars to set our dreams free.
For in this moment, joy fills the air,
In the enchantment of night, we sing and we share.

A Tapestry of Flickering Lights

In the heart of the night, colors ignite,
A tapestry woven, shining so bright.
Under the stars, joy fills the sights,
In the dance of the fire's flickering lights.

Lanterns soar high, painting the sky,
Whispers of laughter, as moments pass by.
Each twinkle a promise, every glow a cheer,
In this feast of warmth, we hold dear.

Songs of the past intertwine with delight,
As we gather together, hearts shining bright.
Through dusk's embrace, we find our way,
Guided by hope that won't fade away.

In this festive night, we weave our dreams,
A tapestry rich, bursting at the seams.
With flickering lights, we cherish the time,
In the beauty of togetherness, we find our rhyme.

The Unknown Among the Light

Twinkling stars dance, a wondrous sight,
Joyful laughter spills into the night.
Colorful lanterns sway in the trees,
Whispers of secrets floated on the breeze.

Children's smiles gleam like gems aglow,
Fireflies swirl, putting on a show.
Happiness blooms in every embrace,
Hearts leap with joy, finding their place.

Music plays softly, a haunting cheer,
Echoes of joy in the atmosphere.
Under the moonlight, dreams take flight,
Celebration pulses, warm and bright.

Every moment cherished, shared delight,
In this festivity, we find our light.
Together we bask in love's sweet glow,
Uncovering mysteries only we know.

Silhouettes of the Night Sky

Silhouettes dance on the canvas vast,
Under a sky where stories are cast.
Stars like diamonds wink and tease,
Illuminating secrets carried with ease.

Fireworks crackle, painting the air,
Colorful bursts, a magical flare.
Joyful hearts echo in rhythmic delight,
Sharing this moment, hearts take flight.

Candles flicker, casting warm spells,
Whispering tales that the nighttime tells.
Each twinkle woven in laughter and play,
As shadows recede, we dance and sway.

Underneath the vast, serenading sky,
We lift our spirits, letting them fly.
In this revelry, we lose all strife,
Embracing the joy that fills our life.

Unveiling the Spectral Veil

Mysteries linger beneath the bright gleam,
As moonbeams flutter, weaving a dream.
Laughter rings out in a jubilant wave,
Chasing the shadows that linger and crave.

Glimmers of magic dance in the air,
Hearts intertwine without a care.
Fires burn bright, stories come alive,
In the embrace of joy, we truly thrive.

A spectral veil lifts, revealing delight,
Colors cascade in the heart of the night.
Every twirl paints a memory bright,
As wishes take flight, shining with light.

Together we'll gather, our spirits ignited,
In the glow of the stars, we're forever delighted.
Hand in hand, through this festive show,
We'll cherish the magic wherever we go.

Beneath the Whispering Vault

Beneath the vault where whispers entwine,
A tapestry woven, fantastically fine.
Swaying together, we lose track of time,
In the soft glow of laughter, life's sweet rhyme.

Bright banners flutter, the air filled with cheer,
As kindred spirits converge, drawing near.
Cheers echo through the vibrant night,
Creating a symphony of pure delight.

Sipping joy from goblets, hearts align,
In the warmth of friendship, we brightly shine.
Together we revel, forgetting our woes,
In the embrace of the magic that flows.

The night unfolds with promises sweet,
As every heartbeat blossoms, we meet.
In the whispers of stars, our hopes take flight,
Forever we'll cherish this dazzling night.

The Night's Tender Touch

The stars twinkle bright, joy in the air,
Soft whispers of laughter, love everywhere.
Dancing shadows sway, in the gentle breeze,
A festive night blooms, hearts at ease.

Lanterns aglow, casting warm light,
Echoes of cheer, lifting spirits high.
Underneath the moon, dreams take their flight,
Embracing the magic that fills the sky.

Songs filled with hope, drift through the trees,
Each note a reminder, of life's sweet tease.
Festive hearts unite, in this wondrous dance,
Together we celebrate, in a joyful trance.

With laughter and cheer, the night carries on,
Under the stars, our worries are gone.
In this tender touch, we find our true bliss,
A moment in time, forever we'll miss.

Whispering Radiance of the Moon

The moon softly glows, casting its spell,
Whispers of light, where magic does dwell.
Gathering dreams, like dew on the ground,
In the night's embrace, pure joy we have found.

Banners of stars, dance high in the night,
Each twinkle a promise, a radiant sight.
Hearts intertwined, beneath this vast dome,
Together we wander, this world feels like home.

Laughter that sparkles, like waves on the sea,
Moments of wonder, shared joyfully.
With every breath drawn, we cherish this tune,
A symphony crafted, by whispers of moon.

As shadows grow long, our tales intertwine,
With festive delight, our spirits align.
In the stillness of night, our hearts take their flight,
Bound by the radiance, of love and of light.

Glistening Reflections of Ascending Dreams

Glistening waters, mirror the bright stars,
Reflections of wishes, dreams held near, not far.
The night unfolds softly, inviting our souls,
To dance in the moonlight, as joy gently rolls.

With each tiny wave, laughter ignites,
A chorus of memories, the heart's pure delights.
Enchanted we move, where shadows cascade,
In the warmth of the moment, our fears start to fade.

Whispers of promise, as dreams take their flight,
Twinkling like fireflies, in the cool of the night.
Gathering together, in celebration so grand,
We cherish this time, hand in hand, we stand.

In the shimmering glow, hope reigns supreme,
With hearts intertwined, we weave a sweet dream.
Glistening reflections, our spirits soar high,
In the festivity's charm, forever we'll fly.

A Harmonious Blend of Light and Shadow

In twilight's embrace, the world starts to gleam,
A dance of soft shadows, ignites every dream.
Laughter and music, a tapestry spun,
In this harmonious night, we revel as one.

The stars weave their stories, a vibrant display,
Echoes of joy, guiding us on our way.
With each gentle murmur, the night comes alive,
In the blend of light, our spirits thrive.

Candle flames flicker, casting warmth all around,
In the festive air, sweet memories abound.
Together we gather, under the radiant sky,
With dreams in our hearts, we let out a sigh.

Through laughter and cheer, this night will remain,
A testament of love, in joy and in pain.
A harmonious blend, where spirits ignite,
In the celebration's glow, we bask in the light.

The Glittering Veil of Secrets

In twilight's embrace, laughter flows bright,
With whispers of joy, the stars take flight.
Colors of joy splashed high in the air,
Veils of glitter dance without a care.

We gather together, hearts warm with light,
Each moment a treasure, everything feels right.
Secrets are shared in the flickering glow,
As bonds intertwine, letting our spirits grow.

Tunes of the night echo soft and sweet,
While twinkling lights beneath our eager feet.
Letting go worries, we revel in bliss,
In the dance of the night, there's magic we miss.

So raise up your glass to the warmth we create,
In this festive spell, we banish all fate.
For tonight we're alive, under starlit skies,
Wrapped in the splendor, where true laughter lies.

An Odyssey Under Moon's Gaze

Beneath the moon's gaze, we start our quest,
With hearts that are lighter, our spirits at rest.
Each step an adventure, each laugh a new tale,
Together we wander, on love's gentle trail.

The sky filled with lanterns, glimmers in sight,
As shadows dissolve, giving way to the night.
With every bright moment, we're spinning with glee,
In this odyssey shared, forever we'll be.

Stars playing music, a sweet serenade,
While dreams rush like rivers, in joy we cascade.
Laughter like fireworks blooms in the air,
A tapestry woven, with love's gentle care.

So here's to the magic that dances around,
To friendships ignited, in silence profound.
On this odyssey bold, with moon's gentle light,
We celebrate together, igniting the night.

Shade and Sparkle in Cosmic Harmony

In the balance of shade, twinkling sparkles gleam,
A dance of the cosmos, a vibrant dream.
We twirl through the night, lost in delight,
While shadows embrace us, holding us tight.

Underneath the starlight, we come alive,
With joy overflowing, together we thrive.
Each flicker a promise, each whisper a tune,
In shade and in sparkle, we worship the moon.

Gathered around fires, where stories are spun,
With laughter that echoes, delight has begun.
In cosmic harmony, we find our own way,
Creating our magic, come night or come day.

With friends by our side, in this world so grand,
In shade and in sparkle, together we stand.
Tonight we are one, with the sky's velvet kiss,
In the warmth of our bonds, we find endless bliss.

Under the Celestial Canopy

Under the canvas of twinkling night,
We gather in joy, hearts soaring in flight.
With laughter like starlight, we light up the sky,
In this celestial dance, our spirits will fly.

The whispers of breezes, secrets they share,
While dreams intertwine in the cool evening air.
With every shared smile, the world feels so right,
In this moment of magic, we sparkle so bright.

As shadows retreat, let the revelry spark,
With echoes of joy that fill up the dark.
In the warmth of our circle, we cherish the now,
To the rhythm of hearts, we take a bold bow.

Under this canopy, our dreams take their flight,
In vibrant celebration, we shine through the night.
With melodies of laughter and love intertwined,
Here under the stars, our souls are aligned.

Secrets Hidden in Soft Radiance

In twilight's glow, the whispers play,
Beneath the stars, where shadows sway.
Dreams sparkle bright, like fireflies dance,
A world of magic, given a chance.

Laughter rings out, a joyous refrain,
As secrets twinkle, like jewels in rain.
Hearts intertwined in festive delight,
Holding the warmth of a starry night.

Colors of joy paint the evening sky,
In every glance, the time slips by.
With every moment, the night reveals,
The beauty of life that gently feels.

So gather near, let your spirit soar,
In this soft radiance, forevermore.
Let secrets bloom like flowers in spring,
In the warmth of light, together we sing.

Dancing in Celestial Haze

Under the moon, we twirl and sway,
Lost in the rhythm of night and day.
Stars above whisper soft and sweet,
As we glide onward, our hearts in beat.

The air is filled with laughter and cheer,
In the celestial haze, we draw near.
Hands held tightly, our spirits take flight,
As the universe beams its radiant light.

Each twinkle a promise, each spin a dream,
In the vastness of night, we find our theme.
With every step, the magic we weave,
In the song of the heavens, we firmly believe.

So dance with me, under stardust skies,
In this moment, let your worries rise.
Together we shimmer, together we shine,
In the haze of the cosmos, your heart is mine.

Light and Shadow Together in Harmony

In the gentle glow of a warm embrace,
Light meets shadow, revealing grace.
In whispers soft, dreams intertwine,
Creating a canvas, exquisite and fine.

Every heartbeat, a rhythmic display,
Under the stars, we find our way.
With laughter echoing, joy takes its flight,
As shadows dance in the glow of the night.

The serenade of life, so richly spun,
A harmony born where two become one.
With every flicker, a story unfolds,
In the festival of life, a treasure of gold.

So join in the dance, let your spirit sing,
In light and shadow, together we bring.
A celebration of being, a beautiful sight,
In the forever fusion of day and night.

Echoes of Twinkling Dreams

In a realm where whispers gently flow,
Twinkling dreams in the moonlit glow.
Each echo carries a memory bright,
Casting a spell in the velvet night.

Voices harmonize under stellar beams,
In the tapestry spun from our wishes and dreams.
With every chuckle, the night unfolds,
Stories of wonder, in laughter retold.

The joy of the moment, a gift to cherish,
As thoughts take flight, they magically flourish.
In the embrace of the night, we find our place,
Wrapped in the wonder, adorned with grace.

So close your eyes and let your heart soar,
In echoes of dreams, forever explore.
For in this festive realm, we undeniably glean,
The magic of life in its vibrant sheen.

Cosmic Whispers Under the Canopy

Stars twinkle bright in the night sky,
Whispers of joy float softly by.
Moonbeams dance on leaves so green,
Nature's chorus, a festive scene.

Laughter echoes through the air,
Fireflies spark with gentle flare.
The world aglow, hearts intertwine,
In this moment, all things align.

Colorful blooms sway with a beat,
Each petal swirls, a rhythmic treat.
The melody of life unfolds,
As every story of love is told.

Under the canopy, we find,
The magic of peace intertwined.
From dusk to dawn, let's celebrate,
In this cosmic dance, it's never too late.

The Ethereal Dance of Ray and Shadow

Sunlight sifts through branches tall,
Creating patterns, a stunning sprawl.
Breezes carry laughter and cheer,
As shadows mingle, drawing near.

Twinkling moments wrapped in gold,
Each memory cherished, never old.
The rhythm of life sings anew,
With every heartbeat, dreams accrue.

Whirls of color in the air,
Joy and music, everywhere.
Like whispers soft from distant stars,
We dance with freedom, forget our scars.

In this festive glow, we reside,
With open arms, hearts open wide.
The ethereal dance, our spirits soar,
Together in harmony, forevermore.

Glimmers of Light in Time's Pause

In the stillness of twilight's embrace,
Glimmers of light emerge with grace.
Each flicker tells a tale of old,
Inviting laughter, warmth, and gold.

The clock stands still, the world in cheer,
Echoes of joy fill the atmosphere.
Beams of hope cast shadows long,
In this moment, we all belong.

Candles flicker with vibrant spark,
Casting radiance against the dark.
Mirth spins in a gentle sway,
As night falls, we find our way.

Under starlit skies, we sing,
Of dreams and hopes that love can bring.
With every glimmer, our hearts entwine,
In this pause of time, joy aligns.

Night's Canvas of Dreams

Night unfolds like a canvas wide,
Where colors of dreams and stars collide.
With whispers soft, the night ignites,
Creating wonders, pure delights.

In gentle hues of silver and blue,
We paint our wishes, bold and true.
Each stroke alive with festive cheer,
In the gallery of night, we're here.

Luminous orbs above us gleam,
Illuminating the fabric of dream.
The moon dances, a radiant queen,
Revealing magic in the unseen.

Gathered 'round in gleeful embrace,
Hearts ignited, spirits interlace.
In this canvas of dreams so bright,
We celebrate love, in the depth of night.

Chasing Shadows of the Night

Beneath the twinkling stars so bright,
We dance with joy, chasing the night.
Laughter echoes through the air,
A festive spirit everywhere.

With every step, the world ignites,
As hearts unite in gleeful sights.
The moon above, a cheerful guide,
Together we celebrate, side by side.

Candles flicker, casting dreams,
In every corner, happiness beams.
So come and join this vibrant throng,
In chasing shadows, we belong.

In joyful whispers, secrets shared,
The warmth of friends, a love declared.
We greet the night with open arms,
Embracing life, its many charms.

The Whispering Light within the Dark

Stars are winking in the sky,
Softly calling, come and fly.
Moonlight dances on the ground,
In whispers sweet, joy can be found.

Festive hearts with every beat,
Twinkling lights, a merry treat.
In the silence, laughter spills,
A symphony of joyous thrills.

Echoes of dreams spark the night,
Filling shadows with pure delight.
In this glow, we find our way,
Together we celebrate today.

Hand in hand, in gentle cheer,
Whispers of love for all to hear.
In every corner, wonder sows,
With every moment, our spirit glows.

Mysteries of the Night Sky

Underneath the vast expanse,
The stars invite us for a dance.
Adventurous hearts in vibrant flow,
Discovering secrets the night can show.

With laughter bright and spirits high,
We gaze in awe at the midnight sky.
Constellations telling tales so bold,
In shimmering stories, joy unfolds.

The Milky Way, a ribbon of dreams,
Awake in wonder, our hearts gleam.
In every twinkle, a wish we send,
As the night wraps us, a festive blend.

United here, our dreams take flight,
In the embrace of the starry night.
Together we wander, hand in hand,
Celebrating the magic of this land.

Flickers of Faith in the Gloom

When shadows cast their gentle sighs,
We find the light behind our eyes.
Candles glow with hope's sweet grace,
In every flicker, a warm embrace.

With hearts aflame, we raise a toast,
To joys discovered, even in most.
In the gloom, we find our way,
With faith that guides us day by day.

The night may seem a canvas dark,
Yet in our hearts, a glowing spark.
Together, we light the way ahead,
With every dream and word we've said.

So gather close, let laughter ring,
In the night, our spirits sing.
Flickers of faith shall always bloom,
In the shadows, we dispel the gloom.

Soft Shimmers of Forgotten Destinies

Beneath the stars, we dance so bright,
In laughter's embrace, hearts alight.
Whispers of dreams take flight on high,
As joy and love share the evening sky.

Candles flicker, shadows play,
In this moment, come what may.
Soft shimmers weave through the air,
Binding us all in festive care.

With every toast, our spirits soar,
Memories cherished, forever more.
The music swells, a jubilant sound,
In this tapestry of love, we're bound.

Let's write our tales in the moon's soft glow,
As the night unfolds, our hearts will know.
Together we weave, hand in hand,
In soft shimmers, we live unplanned.

Echoes of the Infinite Night

Stars twinkle bright in the velvet expanse,
We gather close, lost in the dance.
Laughter rings out like bells from afar,
In this moment, we shine like stars.

The moon casts spells with its silver light,
Every heartbeat a story, pure delight.
In the echoes of joy, our spirits sing,
Unwrapping the wonders that the night will bring.

With every glance, a spark ignites,
As we celebrate the infinite nights.
Hands raise high, with hopes and dreams,
Together, we're more than what it seems.

So let tonight be a canvas wide,
Where memories linger like a joyful tide.
In the echoes of love, let us unite,
Under the spell of the infinite night.

Whispers of Celestial Echoes

In the twilight glow, magic stirs,
Our laughter mingles with soft purrs.
Whispers of stars float through the air,
Enchanting our hearts with a tender care.

The breeze carries secrets, old and sweet,
As we gather round, our circle complete.
Celestial echoes dance through the night,
Binding our souls in shimmering light.

With every heartbeat, stories unfold,
Adventures await, worth more than gold.
We celebrate life with each heartfelt cheer,
Bringing warmth and love, drawing all near.

Under the cosmos, dreams intertwine,
As we bask in magic, kind and divine.
In the whispers of night, we find our way,
Together we shine, come what may.

Glimmers in the Moonlight Veil

Beneath the moon, our spirits rise,
Glimmers of joy paint the skies.
With every glance, the night ignites,
A tapestry woven in love's delights.

Dancing shadows softly twirl,
As friendship blooms, a precious pearl.
In this moment, time stands still,
Embraced by laughter, hearts will fill.

Hand in hand, we chase the stars,
United in dreams, we'll go far.
In the calm of night, together we stand,
With glimmers of hope, our dreams are planned.

With the moon as witness, we make our vow,
In the magic of now, we live and allow.
Below a sky so vast and wide,
In glimmers of joy, forever abide.

Beneath a Canopy of Stars

Beneath the stars, the laughter glows,
With twinkling lights, the night bestows.
We dance beneath the velvet sky,
With dreams alight, our spirits fly.

The whispers of the evening breeze,
Carry joy through the rustling trees.
As friends unite in pure delight,
We celebrate this wondrous night.

Fireflies weave through the glowing air,
Creating magic, beyond compare.
With every smile and every song,
Together is where we all belong.

In joyful hearts, the memories play,
A tapestry of love displayed.
Underneath this starry dome,
We find within, a place called home.

The Dance of Twilight Forms

As daylight fades and shadows creep,
The world awakens from its sleep.
With twilight's brush, the colors blend,
A masterpiece that seems to transcend.

The echoes of the laughter call,
Inside our hearts, we feel the thrall.
With every step, the music sways,
Carving joy through twilight's maze.

The rhythmic beat, a pulse divine,
In every heart, the spark will shine.
With friends around, we hold on tight,
The magic thrums through star-kissed night.

Through dancing forms, we lose all cares,
In unity, our spirit dares.
Together here, our voices blend,
In twilight's arms, we find no end.

Moonlight Caresses the Unknown

Moonlight spills upon the earth,
Awakening dreams of untold worth.
In silken shadows, secrets play,
Guiding our hearts as we drift away.

Whispers of night, a gentle hug,
Pulling us close with its magic tug.
Under the glow, we find our way,
Exploring realms where wishes stay.

Each twinkling star, a tale to tell,
Of distant lands and wishing wells.
Moonlit paths lead us right and true,
Illuminating worlds, all new.

In this embrace, we lose our fears,
With every step, our laughter cheers.
Together we roam, holding the night,
In moonlight's arms, everything feels right.

Glimmers of Light in the Abyss

From deepest dark where shadows dwell,
Glimmers appear like whispered spells.
In the silence, hopes ignite,
Each flicker shines, igniting light.

Dancing flames in the heart's abyss,
Reminding us of the warmth we miss.
Through trials faced, we stand as one,
Together we dream until the dawn.

With every heartbeat, courage grows,
As glimmers of light begin to flow.
In unity, we break the chain,
Transforming darkness into gain.

Through every struggle, joy's rebirth,
In life's sweet chaos, find your worth.
So hold this glow, let it persist,
For in the dark, there waits the bliss.

Ethereal Forms in Midnight's Grasp

In the hush of night's embrace,
Whispers of joy glide and trace.
Stars twinkle like laughter bright,
As dreams take wing in silver light.

Kaleidoscopes swirl in the air,
Colors dancing, free from care.
Hope flutters in each gentle breeze,
As joy unfurls beneath the trees.

Cascades of soft, luminous glow,
Guide hearts where we wish to go.
Echoes of laughter, sweet delight,
Our spirits soar in shared twilight.

Beneath a quilt of velvet skies,
Magic glimmers in our eyes.
In midnight's grasp, we find our place,
In ethereal dreams, we interlace.

Dances of Flickering Silhouettes

Underneath the moon's soft gleam,
We twirl together, lost in dream.
Crisp autumn leaves begin to sway,
As friendships bloom on this bright day.

Shadows stretch like whispers near,
Each flicker dances, loud and clear.
With every step, the world ignites,
In laughter shared, our hearts take flight.

Stars cascade like sparkling rain,
Each twinkle echoes joy's refrain.
A symphony of breath and sound,
In flickering warmth, our joys abound.

Through laughter and the night's embrace,
We find our magic, find our grace.
With flickering silhouettes so bright,
We dance together, hearts alight.

Night's Enchantment of Shadow and Light

In twilight's glow, the world transforms,
With shadows weaving gentle forms.
Candles flicker, soft and low,
As enchantment wraps us slow.

In every corner, laughter sings,
As warmth of twilight gently clings.
A tapestry of dreams unfurled,
In night's embrace, a magic world.

Through whispers shared beneath the stars,
We find our strength, forget our scars.
The dance of light, the shadow's grace,
In this sweet moment, we find our place.

As dawn begins to kiss the night,
We hold the magic, pure and bright.
For in the dusk, we've found our flight,
In night's enchantment of shadow and light.

The Mystique of Dimmed Radiance

In the hush of fleeting hours,
Dimmed radiance softly empowers.
Flickering lights that break the night,
Guide our hearts to pure delight.

The stillness hums with secrets deep,
In this twilight, our spirits leap.
Whispers linger, soft and clear,
As magic draws us ever near.

With every smile, our warmth ignites,
Creating joy through starlit nights.
A dance of shadows, breaths entwined,
In this moment, love defined.

The mystique of dusk, sweet and rare,
Wraps the night with tender care.
In dimmed radiance, we find our way,
To celebrate tomorrow's day.

Secrets of the Celestial Realm

Stars twinkle brightly in the night,
Whispers of wonder, pure delight.
Galaxies dance in the cosmic play,
Magic unfolds as night turns to day.

Moonbeams shimmer on the silver lake,
Dreams awaken, and hearts gently shake.
Mysteries cradle the darkened skies,
Each secret revealed, a sweet surprise.

Comets race with ethereal grace,
In this realm, we find our place.
Voices of old call us to see,
The secrets hidden within the spree.

With every breath, the cosmos sigh,
In every heartbeat, a lullaby.
Festive spirit surrounds us here,
In the celestial realm, we draw near.

Dancing with Celestial Spirits

In the midnight glow, we sway and spin,
With spirits of light, our dance begins.
Stars twirl and weave in ethereal beams,
Painting our laughter with silver dreams.

Galactic echoes laugh and sing,
We join the chorus, a joyous ring.
Through stardust paths, we leap and glide,
With every beat, our hearts collide.

Celestial waltz beneath the moon,
In this celebration, we are in tune.
Floating on notes of a cosmic song,
Together we'll dance the whole night long.

In the dance of time, we find our fate,
With celestial spirits, we celebrate.
The joy of the universe, in every twirl,
In the arms of the night, let the magic unfurl.

Twilight's Canvas of Dreams

Twilight paints the sky with hues so bright,
A canvas adorned with fading light.
Whispers of magic float in the air,
As stars awaken from daytime's snare.

Colors blend in a dreamy swirl,
As hearts ignite in a playful whirl.
Moonlit shadows dance on the ground,
In this magical hour, enchantment is found.

Each star a promise, a wish, a gleam,
In twilight's embrace, we dare to dream.
The world holds its breath, in the soft embrace,
As dreams take flight in this timeless space.

In every corner, joy can be seen,
Painting our lives with a festive sheen.
The twilight whispers of love and cheer,
In the canvas of dreams, we hold dear.

Nebulae in the Whispering Breeze

In the whispering breeze, colors collide,
Nebulae bloom, with secrets inside.
Softly they dance, like petals of light,
Illuminating the dark of the night.

Cosmic wonders spin and twirl,
As stardust mingles in a gentle whirl.
The symphony plays a celestial tune,
Wrapping the world in a silver cocoon.

Floating in dreams, we drift far and wide,
With nebulae's grace, we wander with pride.
Each breath a story, each moment a spark,
In the festive glow of the celestial dark.

Together we sail on the whispering winds,
In this realm of magic, where joy never ends.
Nebulae shine with unspeakable glee,
A celebration of life, wild and free.

www.ingramcontent.com/pod-product-compliance
Ingram Content Group UK Ltd.
Pitfield, Milton Keynes, MK11 3LW, UK
UKHW021605050125
453025UK00007B/82